MR MID-LIFE CRISIS
CRISIS
AND FRIENDS

A Very Unofficial Parody

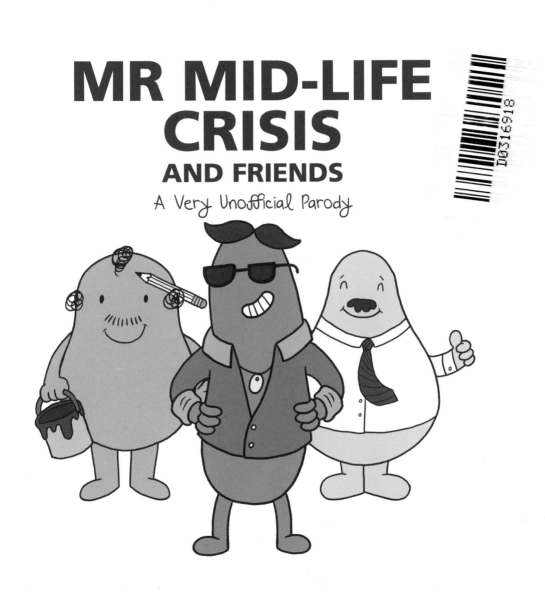

Mr Mid-Life Crisis has just had a big birthday.

He tried to deal with it the modern way; going to a festival, doing a triathlon and having a hair transplant. It didn't make him feel any better. So instead he did it the old-fashioned way. He bought a sports car with the money he and his wife had saved for the new conservatory.

Mr Mid-Life Crisis' wife is doing revenge the old-fashioned way too. She's just covered his sports car with superglue.

Mr Marathon loves running.

He tries to think positive thoughts during each race, but ends up swearing at hills and moaning about his chafed nipples. Afterwards, he feels great – as if he can do anything (apart from walk in shoes that aren't flip-flops).

That's what running is all about. And getting a better time than Simon and Dave from the running club.

Mr Banter is the best Best Man ever.

The stag was a total win. OK, so the groom took a tumble, but they can edit the plaster cast out of the wedding photos, can't they? He's already pranked the groom twice today and slipped four shots of brandy into his morning coffee. Plus his Best Man speech will be HILARIOUS.

Hang on… why is everyone staring at him? What is the groom whispering? … Rings? What rings?

Poor Mr Man Flu has a cold.

It started as a sniffle but now he can feel it in his bones. According to Google, his symptoms are worryingly similar to bird flu. Better stay wrapped up all day. Luckily, his wife is able to look after him, even though she's got her job, their triplets and her elderly mother to care for.

He'd better watch some more "Top Gear" until the medicine kicks in. The sound of the engines is really soothing.

Mr Mamil has taken up a new sport: road cycling.

He's bought all the latest kit; a top of the range bike, a tight lycra onesie and a helmet with a built-in action camera so he can relive his rides.

Today is the first time he has cycled around the park. Usually he rides around the pond in his garden, or polishes the bike in his garage. One day he might actually try cycling on the road.

Mr Box Set Bore once led a very different life.

He used to play football and go to the pub. He talked to people and even read books. Now, he watches box sets. Tonight, he is watching "The Killing". He's done the maths and he'll be able to do the whole first season in one night.

The next morning, he opens the bathroom door violently in case there's a serial killer behind it, and says thank you to the newsagent in Danish.

Mr Dad Dancer loves a party.

Wherever there's music and a floor to dance on he's ready to show off his moves, from the "Hand Clap Boogie" and "Whistling Shuffle", to the "Side Step Slide".

He does not care what anyone else thinks. He just wants to have a good time and, more importantly, to totally embarrass his kids. After all, that is what being a parent is all about.

Mr Geek cannot wait for Comic Con.

He has bought his tickets, planned the panels to attend and picked the stars he wants to meet. Now… what to wear? He checks out the cosplay forum. There is a heated discussion thread between the Thronies and the Trekkies. He can't decide whether he's #TeamJon or #TeamSpock.

In the end he decides to go as Jon Spock. Now that is a crossover he can really get behind.

Mr DIY loves his shed.

It is full of things that only he finds useful. Like jam jars filled with rusting screws, tins stuffed with Allen keys, broken tools and bits of wood to stir paint with.

He loves DIY projects too. Today he is making a porthole window for his shed out of the washing machine door. His wife is going to be so pleased, especially when he wins Shed of the Year.

Mr Middle Age is worried it is too late.

He spent his youth enjoying himself and having fun. Now that he is approaching the big Five-0, he has noticed a wrinkle or three, not to mention his disappearing hairline.

He looks at the bathroom shelf. What was that stuff his wife told him to put under his puffy eyes? Toothpaste? That's it. Yes, he's sure that's what she said. It's not too late... is it?

Mr Competitive Dad often gets carried away.

He forgets that he does not know more than the referee. And that it is not necessary to invade the pitch, steal the ball from a seven year old child, score the goal and then run around the pitch with his jumper over his head.

Soon, it will be the school sports day. Time to implement his daily training schedule for the egg and spoon race… can't have Junior coming in second place again.

Mr Townie and his family live in the country now.

They have never been happier since they left the city. All those beautiful fields and country lanes. And trees. And mud. And more trees.

He fits in well with the locals too. It was a bit of a shock to discover there was nowhere he could get a decaf mocha soy latte at night, but if he drives really fast it only takes him three-and-a-half hours to get back to London.

Mr Hipster is finally living the dream.

Once he was just Phil from accounts, but one day he wandered into an organic artisanal doughnut shop, and he never looked back. It took a while to grow his facial hair, but he stuck at it until he could fashion an intricate moustache-and-beard combo that has to be soaked in honeybee nectar every night.

The upcycled retro bike took a bit of getting used to. But now he thinks he cuts quite a dash on his way into the office.

Mr Hangry's meeting started over two hours ago.

There's plenty of tea and coffee in the board room, but no BISCUITS. He knows there are BISCUITS. He saw them on a plate outside. But despite this, no one has brought them in yet.

All Mr Hangry can think about is BISCUITS. For the past hour he has been blaming his rumbling stomach on airplanes. Being hungry is making him angry. If someone doesn't do something soon he is going to… oh, here's Andy with the BISCUITS. That's better.

Mr Commuter quite likes his train journey.

It's true that it takes him three hours each way, but he does have a lovely house in the country. It is a shame that he only gets to sleep there. But the train is his sanctuary. He plays lots of stimulating games on his phone. Sometimes, to cheer himself up, he watches people who got on after him struggling to find a seat.

It is the small things in life really, isn't it?